Windsurfing Sports

Amanda Barker • • • • • • • • • •

Heinemann LIBRARY

www.heinemann.co.uk

Visit our website to find out more information about **Heinemann Library** books.

To order:
☎ Phone 44 (0) 1865 888066
▤ Send a fax to 44 (0) 1865 314091
💻 Visit the Heinemann Bookshop at www.heinemann.co.uk to browse our catalogue and order online.

First published in Great Britain by Heinemann Library, Halley Court, Jordan Hill, Oxford OX2 8EJ, a division of Reed Educational and Professional Publishing Ltd.

Heinemann is a registered trademark of Reed Educational & Professional Publishing Limited.

OXFORD   MELBOURNE   AUCKLAND
JOHANNESBURG   BLANTYRE   GABORONE
IBADAN   PORTSMOUTH NH (USA)   CHICAGO

Designed by Celia Floyd
Illustrations by Jeff Edwards
Originated by HBM Print, Singapore
Printed in Hong Kong by Wing King Tong

ISBN 0 431 03679 9 (hardback)
04 03 02 01 00
10 9 8 7 6 5 4 3 2 1

ISBN 0 431 03688 8 (paperback)
04 03 02 01 00
10 9 8 7 6 5 4 3 2 1

British Library Cataloguing in Publication Data

Barker, Amanda
  Windsurfing. – (Radical sports)
  1. Windsurfing – Juvenile literature
  I. Title
  797.3'3

Acknowledgements

The Publishers would like to thank the following for permission to reproduce photographs:

David Eberlin, pp. 15 top, 24, 25, 27 right;
RYA, p. 4, p. 5, p. 18 (Mike O'Brien), p. 26 (Peter Bentley), p. 27 left;
SPORT. The Library, pp. 8, 9, 10, 11, 19 (Robert Armstrong), 20, 21, 22 (Tim McKenna), 23 (Col Stewart), 29 top (Rudiger Faessel)
SSM Freesports, p. 28;
Steve Behr, pp. 6-7, 12-13, 14, 15 bottom, 16-17;
Vandystadt/Allsports, p.29 bottom.

Cover photograph reproduced with permission of Yann Guichaona/Vandtstadt/Allsport.

Our thanks to Gillian Horne of the Royal Yachting Association for her comments in the preparation of this book. Thanks also to Catherine and Richard Potter for appearing in the technique photographs and to Guy Chilvers at Bic Sport UK for his help and loan of the equipment. Thanks to the staff at Willen Lake for the use of their facilities.

Every effort has been made to contact copyright holders of any material reproduced in this book. Any omissions will be rectified in subsequent printings if notice is given to the Publisher.

Any words appearing in the text in bold, **like this**, are explained in the Glossary.

This book aims to cover all the essential techniques of this radical sport but it is important when learning a new sport to get expert tuition and to follow any manufacturers' instructions.

CONTENTS

INTRODUCTION

A short history

Windsurfing is a radical new sport that has grown in popularity since the 1960s. Exactly who invented the windsurfing board has been heavily debated. The first ever sailboard was reported in a science magazine in 1965; this new invention was designed by an American called Newman Darby. It was little more than a floating platform with a fixed sail attached to it.

However, it is two Californians, Jim Drake and Hoyle Schweizer, who are generally credited as the inventors of the sailboard in 1969. Schweizer patented their 'freesailing system' in many countries to stop others copying their design. This patent was contested in the UK by Peter Chilvers, an Englishman who claimed to have invented and used a sailboard in 1958. The judge upheld his claim and, as far as the UK was concerned, Chilvers became the inventor of the sailboard. By 1970 the first manufactured boards went on sail and interest in the sport boomed.

What set sailboards apart from dinghies was the fact that the sail could spin round on its **mast foot**. This was made possible by the use of a special device known as the **UJ** (Universal Joint).

Early windsurfers in the 1970s used **long boards** with floppy sails. They relied on their own strength as the harness had not yet been developed.

Increasing popularity

By the 1990s windsurfing had become a popular sport with around half a million regular sailors in the UK alone. It has a cool image and attracts young and old, female and male alike. Most enthusiastic beginners can learn quickly and soon master the basic skills. Modern boards and **rigs** are light, **buoyant** and easy to handle. Equipment is reasonably cheap, especially if second hand.

Modern sails are lighter than those used in the 1970s. The sailor can travel much faster using a harness to **sheet in** and create power.

Why windsurf?

First, it helps keep you fit. Second, windsurfing presents a new challenge to every level of sailor. There is always some new skill to learn, whether it's learning to go faster or mastering the latest radical **freestyle** move. Windsurfing is an exciting sport in which you can really test your own skills as well as have fun with like-minded people.

The board

People new to the sport of windsurfing usually want to master the basics of the sport quickly. It's important to learn using the right equipment. The main thing to consider as a learner is the stability of the board. Most beginner boards have plenty of volume, which means that they will float even when carrying the heaviest sailor. This enables new sailors to progress quickly.

The one for you

Boards with a volume of 120–160 litres and a length of around 310–330 centimetres are ideal for younger people but would probably be too small for the average sized adult to learn on. There are also special **rigs** produced for children – these are smaller in size and lighter in weight. The **mast** and **boom** are also narrower to fit small hands.

Sail

Sails come in many sizes and shapes. Learners' sails don't tend to have **battens** so they are lighter and easier to use in light winds. However, as you improve a battened sail will give you more stability in stronger winds.

Boom

Modern booms are light as they are made from metal and carbon. They adjust to fit different sized sails. They are easily attached to the mast using a clamp. The boom should be set at shoulder height.

Uphaul rope

The **uphaul** rope is used to pull the sail out of the water.

Mast and mast foot

The mast is attached to the board by the **mast foot**. The mast foot contains a **UJ** which clicks into the **mast track** or **deckplate**. The UJ allows the rig to bend or to be held at any angle. You steer the board in this way. Modern masts contain carbon, making them very light.

Daggerboard

The **daggerboard** is a large moveable plate that helps to keep the board stable and stops it from moving sideways. It can be retracted when the wind blows up, to help keep control of the board. Advanced boards, being shorter, don't have daggerboards but all long raceboards do.

Harness lines

Harness lines are used by improving sailors in stronger winds. They link you to the rig. They should be carefully set to the balance point of the boom. This helps to take pressure off your arms.

Fin or skeg

The fin or skeg is attached to the underside of the board and helps keep the board sailing in a straight line. It also produces lift, which makes the board travel faster.

Footstraps

These are only used by advanced sailors using the harness when **blasting** along at top speed. Footstraps provide anchorage and control in **planing** conditions.

SAFETY FIRST

Always check the condition of kit before sailing. Make sure the rope is not frayed and is firmly secured, and that the rig and boom are firmly attached. After sailing rinse the kit with fresh water and check for damage.

WHAT GEAR DO YOU NEED?

Windsurfing is great fun in sunny weather. It may be tempting to sail in a bathing costume but this is not sensible. Sunburn should be avoided at all times using a high protection water-resistant cream. In colder climates, keeping warm is the main consideration. Whatever the weather you should be properly kitted out for the conditions of the day.

Buoyancy aid

This is an essential piece of kit. A buoyancy aid will keep you afloat and confident. It must fit properly and not be loose. In some places you're not allowed to sail without one. A buoyancy aid is not a life jacket. It will not necessarily float you face-up if you are knocked unconscious. Only a life jacket will do this, but life jackets are too bulky for windsurfing.

Wetsuit

A wetsuit is essential when sailing in cooler seas or inland waters. Wetsuits are made from neoprene. There are different types of suits for summer and winter. Many centres hire them out. A wetsuit and shoes are usually the first pieces of equipment people purchase. Whether you buy it new or second-hand, a wetsuit should fit snugly against your body in order to keep you warm.

Rubber boots or slip-on shoes

Special windsurfing shoes are not necessary to start with – an old pair of trainers will do. Windsurfing shoes are made of **neoprene** and have rubber soles with a strong grip. They stop you from slipping around and also protect your feet from cuts and grazes.

Gloves

Gloves for warmth are only necessary in the winter but some sailors wear them to protect their fingers and palms from blisters. Rubber washing-up gloves are a cheap alternative! Most advanced sailors prefer to sail without as they find gloves affect their grip.

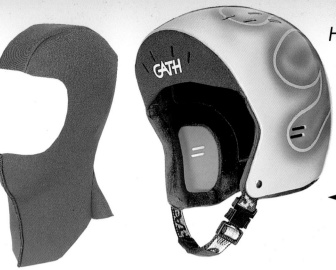

Hats and helmets

Helmets are worn for safety by speed sailors – the faster they go the harder they fall! In winter many people wear neoprene balaclavas to keep warm. On a cold day most body heat is lost through the head.

Harness

This accessory is not essential for a beginner. There are three main types of harness on the market: chest, seat and waist. Before buying one it's best to try out a few to see which feels most comfortable. The harness has a hook in the middle, which attaches you to the harness lines. This takes the weight off your arms when sailing in **planing** conditions.

SAFETY FIRST

- Never sail without wearing a buoyancy aid.

- Never sail without insurance cover. It's often compulsory if sailing on inland water.

- Never sail where there is no rescue service available.

- Attach a tether to your **mast foot** until you have mastered turning.

TOP TIP

- Items that should be carried in a bum bag:
  • spare rope
  • 4-metre towing line
  • fluorescent flag
  • whistle

- You should also carry a penknife and flares.

KEEPING FIT

Although windsurfing is a sport for everyone, keeping fit has obvious advantages. Strength is not the most important factor – stamina and suppleness need most attention. Windsurfing exercises the muscles so it is important that they are warmed up before sailing.

Warming up

During a warm-up pay particular attention to your back, shoulders and arms. This will improve your flexibility on the water. Stretching should be done slowly and gently and should not cause any pain. You should also do some cooling down exercises after your sailing session to stop you aching the next day.

Back and thigh stretch

Bring one knee up and hold it in this position for 10 seconds. Then do the same with the other leg.

Back stretch

Hold your hands behind your back and gently stretch upwards and outwards.

Calf stretch

Stand with feet together and stretch towards your toes. Hold this stretch for 10 seconds.

Inner thigh stretch

Sit down with one leg straight out in front of you and one bent behind you. Reach for the ankle of your front leg. Hold this stretch for 10 seconds then swap legs.

Hamstring stretch

Bend one leg up behind you and gently hold it there for 10 seconds. Then swap legs.

Leg stretch ·················

Stand with one leg bent in front of you and one leg straight behind you. Gently lean forward on your bent leg to feel the stretch in the rear leg. Hold this for 10 seconds then swap legs,

······· **Neck stretch**

Hold onto your head and gently bring it towards your right shoulder. Hold this for 10 seconds before slowly straightening up and bringing it towards your left shoulder.

Building stamina

Endurance training helps you to prepare for long spells on the water. Running, cycling, rowing and swimming can all help to build stamina. These activities can be carried out all year round.

Increasing strength

Time on the water is the best way to build up the muscles needed for windsurfing. There are other ways of building strength but it's not advisable for young people, under 16 years old, to weight train as this can damage their bones. Supervised training in the gym is all right so long as it does not involve lifting weights.

SAFETY FIRST

- Don't allow yourself to become exhausted or **dehydrated** when sailing.

- Dehydration can be a problem in the summer. On hot days aim to drink about a litre of water every two hours.

- Make sure you're fit enough to cope with the day's weather conditions.

The right food

Eating a healthy diet is important too. Food creates the energy that increases stamina and endurance. Chips and cola don't provide sustained energy – bananas and water do a better job.

LAUNCHING THE BOARD

Starting off

Getting onto a board and staying on is often the trickiest skill to master. But, with determination and a sense of humour success is guaranteed!

The board is stable when the hands are placed either side of the mast.

To start with practise getting on and off a board in waist-deep water. Make sure the **daggerboard** is pushed down to help keep the board stable. Place your hands either side of the **mast foot** over the **centreline**, then raise your body onto the board in a kneeling position. Stand up slowly, keeping your weight over the centreline, and your feet either side of the mast foot. Practise moving up and down the board, turning around and standing on one leg.

Kneeling over the centreline stops you from tipping into the water.

Grasp the **uphaul** rope in both hands and slowly pull the sail out of the water.

The next step

Once in the central kneeling position, take hold of the uphaul rope. Next, holding onto the rope and facing into the sail, get into a crouching position. Slowly rise to stand with your knees slightly bent, pulling the rope as you go. Take hold of the mast and relax, keeping your arms and legs slightly bent. Now you're ready to sail.

Beach starting

As you progress you will learn new skills. It doesn't take long to master beach starting. This is done in shallow water. First, set the position of the board and **rig**. Next, place your back foot on the board and when the sail catches the wind step neatly up and sail away!

Beach starting is practised in windier conditions; the sail is positioned to catch the wind.

GOOD STANCE

The way the windsurfer stands on the board is known as stance. Good stance from the very start is important for the following reasons. First, it helps to save energy, which means that longer periods can be spent on the water. Second, good stance protects you from injury. Many beginners can certainly feel their back muscles at the end of a day on the water. Finally, a good stance helps you to control the power in the sail using your body weight.

What is good stance?

Notice the following important factors.

- The **rig** is more or less upright.
- Your head is looking forward, in the direction the board is sailing.
- Your arms are slightly bent and hands are shoulder width apart on the **boom**.
- Your upper body is straight.
- You're leaning backwards a little to balance the power in the sail.
- Your feet are behind the **mast foot**, your front foot is pointing towards the direction of sailing and your back foot is at a right angle to the edge of the board.

Notice how the arms are straight and the shoulders are tilted back. The legs are slightly bent and the butt is tucked in.

SAFETY FIRST

- Never sail if you're the only person on the water!
- Always inform someone of your plans and expected time of return.

When sailing fast

As you improve and your sailing speeds get faster, your feet will be positioned further back down the board. A harness will have become an essential piece of equipment by now and the next step is to get your feet into the footstraps. Good stance is essential at this level, without it those wild **blasting** sessions are impossible. The sailing position can be likened to sitting on a high stool – your head should be positioned as if you were trying to look around the other side of the **mast**.

Steering

Steering a windsurfer is rather like steering a bike. To turn towards the wind steer the rig towards the back of the board; to turn away from the wind lean the rig towards the front. As you improve your technique your feet should be used to steer the board. This involves transferring your body weight onto your heels or toes. If you move your weight onto your back foot you will help bury the edge of the board in the water and it will start to turn.

It's always important to look in the direction you are steering.

When sailing at speed the shoulders are leaning outwards to balance the power in the sail.

TACKING

Turning the front of the board through the **eye of the wind** is called **tacking**. Tacking a board is necessary when sailing **upwind**. The beginner's tack is basically the same as a more advanced move. An advanced tack is carried out at speed.

The beginner's tack

The first step when starting to tack is to move your front hand onto the **mast**. At the same time, move your front foot just in front of the **mast foot**. The **clew** is leant to the back of the board.

Notice how the front foot has been moved in front of the mast, the front hand has also been moved and the sail is tilted to the back of the board.

As the board turns through the wind you start to shuffle round to the other side of the sail.

The board turns towards the wind and as it moves through the eye of the wind you swap position. Shuffle round the mast to the other side, swapping your hands and feet, so that you end up facing the other way.

To complete the tack the sailor steps round to the other side of the board and takes hold of the **boom** again.

Advanced tacking

The advanced tack is a graceful and rapid move. Rather than shuffling slowly around the front of the board you hop round as the nose passes through the eye of the wind, keeping your body low and arms fairly straight.

An advanced sailor can complete the turn quickly.

SAFETY FIRST

- Never sail where there is no rescue cover available.

- Attach a **tether** to your **mast foot** until you have mastered turning.

GYBING

When a windsurfer **gybes** the back of the board turns through the wind. Gybing is carried out when sailing **downwind**. Downwind sailing is carried out with the wind behind you and is called '**running** with the wind'. You may think that sailing on a run is the quickest way to sail. In fact, this is not the case – sailing on a **reach** gives more speed.

The beginner's gybe

Before starting to gybe you must be on a run with the sail at right angles to the **rig**. In a gybe the sail is flipped round the front of the board. Gybing is a quicker way to turn the board but it can result in you being carried further **upwind**.

This sailor is starting to gybe. The sail is beginning to flip round to the front of the board.

Flare gybe

As you progress to sailing in stronger winds, gybing will become a faster and more dynamic move. At this stage it is called a **flare gybe**. The tail of the board is sunk using foot pressure (applied by the weight of your body) and the rig flip is carried out with more speed.

Carve gybe

The **carve gybe** is the one skill that most windsurfers aim to achieve. It's carried out at great speed in **planing** conditions. Carving a board through the wind is very graceful. The sailor is truly surfing as the turn is carried out. There are, of course, even more tricks to learn once this skill has been perfected. In **freestyle** events sailors have shown off **monkey** and even **aerial gybes**!

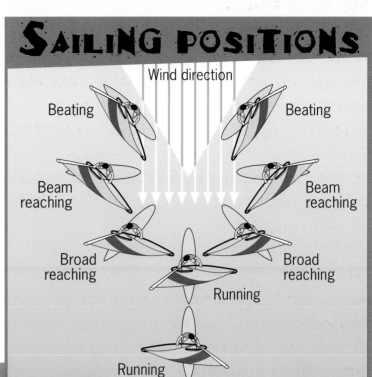

SAILING POSITIONS

Wind direction

Beating

Beating

Beam reaching

Beam reaching

Broad reaching

Broad reaching

Running

Running

SAFETY

- Always check the weather forecast before you go out sailing.

- Avoid sailing in the sea if the wind is blowing off shore.

- Never sail if the visibility is poor or it's close to sunset.

- Choose a landmark on the shore and keep checking your position against it to stop yourself drifting downwind.

WHEN THINGS GO WRONG

Wipeouts

Every windsurfer, even the most skilled, falls off!
Spectacular falls are known as **wipeouts** and most
sailors enjoy telling tales of their experiences.
Windsurfers are lucky because falling into the water is
usually less painful than falling onto solid ground.
Despite this, it's important that every sailor knows what to
do in an emergency.

Getting help

It's foolish to sail in places where there is no rescue
cover. If you get into difficulty on the water, for whatever
reason, the sensible thing to do is wave for help. There
are a number of ways you can attract the attention of a
rescue boat.

- Sitting safely on the
  board, raise both hands
  over your head, then
  lower them. Do this
  repeatedly. This is known
  as the international
  distress signal.
- If you have a fluorescent
  coloured flag in your
  safety pack wave it.
- If there is a whistle
  attached to your
  buoyancy aid blow it in
  short bursts.

Sitting on the board close to the
mast, the sailor repeatedly raises
and lowers both his arms to attract
attention.

Helping yourself

If there is no sign of help and no rescue cover available, there are ways in which you can rescue yourself. These should only be used as a last resort. In light winds the 'butterfly method' can be carried out. Lay the sail across the back of the board and lie on top of this facing towards the nose. Then paddle in towards the shore using your hands. The **rig** should be held in place by your bodyweight.

The butterfly method can be used in light winds.

In stronger winds it might be necessary to unfasten the rig from the board. **De-rigg** the sail and roll it around the **mast**. Lie on top of the rolled-up sail and paddle towards the shore. Both methods of self-rescue can be tricky and should be practised in shallow water.

Self-rescue should only be done as a last resort.

SAFETY

- Never separate yourself from the board if the rig comes free – the board is **buoyant**, the sail isn't.

- Make sure you are capable of sailing in the present wind conditions. This will cut down the likelihood of you having to be rescued.

- Carry a safety pack.

RiDiNG THe WAVeS

Essential skills

Wave sailing is the most radical and advanced type of windsurfing. You should never attempt this unless you can do all of the following things confidently.

- You must be able to **waterstart** the board every time, not just occasionally.
- You must be able to use a **short board** comfortably, **hooked in** and **blasting** along with your feet firmly in the footstraps.

Where are the waves?

The best waves for this type of sailing are found on coastlines open to the oceans. Most of today's top sailors grew up in places such as Hawaii and Australia where the beaches are pounded by ocean rollers. However, it's possible to learn to ride the waves and to jump anywhere in the world. Wave chop on an inland lake can provide enough lift to learn the basics of wave jumping.

Leaping into the air off a wave takes a lot of nerve!

Tricky moves

Wave sailing involves catching a wave just before it breaks. The aim is to ride along the face of the wave in a line as a surfer would do.

Windsurfers have learned how to do tricks on the waves too. They can lift themselves high into the air to perform forward and backward loops. The **tabletop** is another airborne trick performed by the best. Other tricks such as the **body drag** and the **willy skipper** are carried out while sailing in a straight line, but not usually when riding a wave.

Australian Jessica Crisp in the Aloha Classic Competition in 1991.

SAFETY FIRST

- Wave sailors should never sail off rocky beaches or where there are strong **rip currents**.

- Remember who has right of way on the sea. The most important rule is that when two craft are sailing on the same **tack**, the craft on the **windward** side should give way. Generally, larger boats, particularly those with motors, should give way to a windsurfer.

- Never sail close to harbours or shipping lanes, or to where people are swimming.

TAKING IT FURTHER

Where to start

Finding a place to start has never been easier. There are windsurfing schools both on the coast and inland in every continent. National organizations such as the Royal Yachting Association in the UK produce a *Centres Brochure*, which lists centres nationwide. They also advertise in windsurfing magazines and on the Internet. The basics of the sport can be learned in a few short lessons with the most suitable kit. Courses are usually held during the main school vacations and throughout the summer period.

Windsurfing clubs

Joining a local club is another popular way to start out. This has the added appeal of meeting like-minded people, and windsurfers are usually the friendliest people around. Clubs are also a good source of cheap second-hand kit, and experienced windsurfers are always around to give advice about what board or sail to buy.

Learning a new sport helps you to meet other people with similar interests.

Holidays in the sun

Some people are not lucky enough to live in places where the sun is hot and the summers are long. They might prefer to learn abroad on a specialist windsurfing holiday. Every level of sailor is catered for as expert tuition and top-level kit are provided. Most people find that they improve in leaps and bounds in just a few days. Details can be found in travel agents, in magazines and on the Internet.

Many holiday resorts cater for people who want to learn how to windsurf. They provide both tuition and rescue cover.

WINDSURFING LOCATIONS

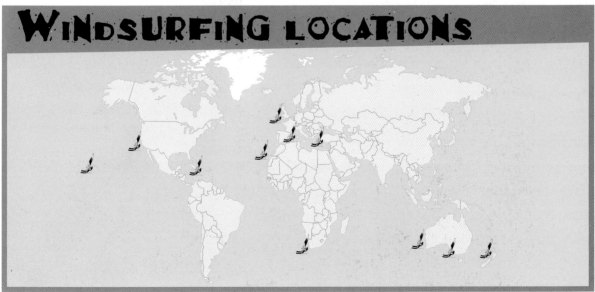

STARTING TO COMPETE

The benefits

Competitive sailing is the way forward for many improvers. Events for amateurs are held both on lakes and the sea. Competitions offer the chance to check out new sailing venues and to compare your skills with others of the same age. There are always experts and new friends on hand to give advice. Competition sailing includes speed and course racing, **freestyle** and wave sailing.

Beginners' events

There are special classes for young sailors who want to race. Those aged under 13 are encouraged to start in the **Junior One Design Fleet** and the **103 Fleet**. Once they feel confident and have grown enough to handle a longer board they move up to the **Aloha Fleet**. Racers in the same event use identical boards so that the winner has no kit advantage.

Here the racing windsurfers are tacking around a marker buoy, the key is to turn as close to the buoy as you can.

Talented young sailors are often spotted at these competitions and may be given the opportunity to train with a regional squad. In the UK the Royal Yachting Association has a strong youth training programme and can advise kids on how to get into racing.

Events in Australia

Australia has its own system of junior racing using the Bombora One Design board.

Increased competition

Other classes of competition are more suited to **short board** sailors. Freestyle events are all about who can show off the trickiest moves. Slalom racing involves either sailing a figure-of-eight course or round a series of buoys on a **downwind** course. Speed sailing is timed over a straight-line course, which is usually 100 metres for amateurs. Sailors blast along between the two points, and everyone is allowed more than one go.

FIND OUT MORE

- Find out about racing from magazines and the Internet

- Join an organization such as the United Kingdom Board Sailing Association (UK), British Windsurfing Association (UK), Australian Yachting Association (Australia) or United States Boardsailing Association (USA).

A freestyle sailor performs a rail ride manoeuvre.

It's never too early to start competing, there are competitions for all ages and abilities.

The world tour

The very best sailors are sponsored and windsurf for a living. Professionals take part in their own competitions. The PWA (Professional Windsurfing Association) runs a world tour every year. Most events take place on **short boards** and some sailors even have their own custom-built boards. The tour visits the widest and windiest windsurfing spots, such as Hawaii, the Canary Islands and the Caribbean. These events are filmed and can be seen on cable and satellite TV. Windsurfing became an Olympic event in 1984.

Indoor sailing

Indoor sailing is also part of the world tour. Huge fans create artificial wind and the sailors **blast** around a short course. They use ramps to give them lift and then show off their most radical loops and twists. Speed sailing generally takes place on flat water. At international level this is timed over a 500-metre course. In 1998 the fastest speed recorded was over 80 kph.

Professional sailors are sponsored by big companies. Here they are taking part in a race at one of the specially chosen windy venues – the Greek Island of Paros.

Who are the international stars?

Most professional sailors started when they were kids. Bjorn Dunkerbeck was still in his twenties when he became World Champion for the eleventh time. He grew up in the Canary Islands and spent all his free time in the sea.

Robbie Naish is the other superstar of windsurfing. He has been on the PWA world tour since it began in the early 1980s and is probably the most well-known windsurfer in the world! He grew up on the Hawaiian Island of Maui, legendary for its huge waves. Not surprisingly, Robbie is the king of wave sailing.

The picture above helps to explain why Dunkerbeck has been World Champion so many times.

Robbie Naish is the grand master of windsurfing.

Natalie Lelievre at the first indoor competition in Paris in 1990.

Windsurfing has its women stars too. Karin Jaggi of Switzerland and Natalie Lelievre of France are two women to watch.

There are many up-and-coming faces on the scene. The stars of tomorrow are the beginners of today, so get on that board and practise!

GLOSSARY

103 Fleet   a racing class for young sailors (under 13 years) using a one-design long board

aerial gybe   a gybe performed in mid-air

Aloha Fleet   a racing class for the one design long race boards, suitable for experienced juniors

batten   a strip of fibreglass inserted into the sail to help keep its shape

blasting   sailing at full speed

body drag   holding onto the rig and sailing along with your feet trailing in the water

boom   used by sailors to hold the rig. It stretches the sail and stops it from flapping. The harness lines are attached to the boom

buoyant   the ability to float

carve gybe   an advanced top speed gybe achieved by foot steering

centreline   runs along the middle of the board from nose to tail. The daggerboard is set along the centreline

clew   the outermost corner of the sail

daggerboard   a large moveable fin set directly behind the mast. It helps to keep the board stable

deckplate   see mast track

dehydration   when the body is deprived of fluid

de-rigging   taking apart the mast, boom and sail

downwind   sailing in the same direction as the wind, with the wind blowing from behind you

duck tack   a freestyle of tacking where the sailor ducks under the rig as the board turns

eye of the wind   the direction the wind is blowing from

flare gybe   an intermediate gybe performed by sinking the tail in the water

freestyle   performing tricks on a board

gybe   turning the board so that the tail passes through the eye of the wind

hooked in   sailing with the harness attached to the harness lines

Junior One Design Fleet   a long racing board designed for sailors under 13 years old

long board   usually a board with a length of over 300 centimetres

mast   supports the front edge of the sail

mast foot   a device that connects the mast to the board and includes the UJ

mast track   the mast is fixed onto the board by plugging the UJ into the mast track or deckplate. This is situated in the middle of the board. There are usually several positions in which the mast can be set onto the deckplate depending on the wind strength.

monkey gybe   a freestyle of gybe that includes a 360-degree rig flip

neoprene   a special material made from rubber

nose-sink tack   a freestyle of move that involves sinking the front of the board as it tacks

planing   sailing at such a speed that the board skims over the water with its nose in the air

reaching   sailing across the wind

rig   the mast, sail and boom

rigging   assembling the mast, sail and boom

rip current   a current that flows out to sea and is capable of carrying a board away from the shore

running   sailing with the wind directly behind you

sheeting in   pulling the sail in with the backhand, to increase power and speed

sheeting out   pushing the sail out with the backhand, to decrease power and speed

short board   usually a board with a length less than 300 centimetres

tabletop   an extreme aerial wave manoeuvre where the underside of the board is turned to face the sky

tacking   sailing a zigzag course upwind, or turning the board so that the nose passes through the eye of the wind

UJ   short for universal joint, a device that fits into the mast foot and enables the rig to be tilted

uphaul   a rope attached to the front edge of the boom, used to pull the rig out of the water. Also, the action of pulling the rig out of the water

upwind   travelling against the wind direction (although it is impossible to sail directly into the wind, it is possible to sail at an angle of around 45 degrees to the wind)

waterstart   a way of getting going in deep water without having to uphaul

willy skipper   an advance freestyle move that involves spinning the board through 180 degrees to land, sailing backwards

windward   on the side from which the wind is blowing

wipeout   a spectacular fall while sailing

USEFUL ADDRESSES

RYA Windsurfing
RYA House
Romsey Road
Eastleigh
Hampshire
SO50 9YA
E-mail: windsurfing@rya.org.uk
tel: 01703 627496
fax: 01703 627482

(long board racing)
United Kingdom Board Sailing Association
PO Box 28
Fareham
Hampshire
PO14 3XD
tel: 01329 664779
fax: 01329 665728

(slalom, wave, speed)
British Windsurfing Association
Mengham Cottage
Mengham Lane
Hayling Island
Hants
PO11 9JX
E-mail: britishwindsurfing@compuserve.com
tel/fax: 01705 468182

United States Boardsailing Association
PO Box 206
Oyster Bay
NY 117711

Canadian Yachting Association
333 River Road
Vanier
Ottawa
Ontario
K1L 8B9

Australian Yachting Federation
33 Peel St
Milson's Point
NSW 2061

New Zealand Yachting Federation
PO Box 4173
Auckland

FURTHER READING

Magazines

Windsurf, Arcwind Ltd
Boards, Boards Ltd

Videos (from RYA)

Windsurfing Fundamentals (W44A) Levels 1–3
Turn for the Better (W45A, W47A) Levels 4-5

Books

Learn to Windsurf, Bill Dawes, Ward Lock
Windsurfing: Step-by-step to success, Rob Reichenfield, The Crowood Press

Websites

www.boards.co.uk
www.zagato.demon.co.uk/bwa
www.sailing.org/imco/
www.world-windsurfing.com
www.americanwindsurfer.com

INDEX